Shoes for Lucy

by Lynne Kemen

Southern Collective Experience
www.southerncollectiveexperience.com

Copyright © 2023 by Lynne Kemen

All rights reserved. No part of this book may be reproduced or transmitted in any form or by any means, electronic or mechanical, including photocopying, recording, or any information storage and retrieval system, without permission in writing from the publisher.

ISBN: 978-1-7362306-4-0

Printed in the United States of America

This paper meets the requirements of ANSI/NISO Z39.48-1992

(Permanence of Paper)

Cover Design and formatting by Kaitlyn Young

Praise for *Shoes for Lucy*

Lynne Kemen's *Shoes for Lucy* is an ambitious collection with topics ranging from the loss of a life partner to childhood recollections to ekphrastic poems. With a keen eye for detail and a well-tuned ear for sonic structure, she crafts direct, engaging poems. These are poems I will return to often for their honesty, humor, and humanness.

- Malaika King Albrecht,
Inaugural Heart of Pamlico Poet Laureate and author of 4 poetry books.

Shoes for Lucy draws us in, line by exquisite line. We return again and again to its beauty in search of authenticity. When we close the last page of our first read of this spellbinding collection where nothing of grief is airbrushed, we too are clear-eyed about life, and with Lynne Kemen and her memory of Nathan Cohen, owner of The Last Wound-Up toy store in New York City on Columbus Avenue, we are singing: *"Carpe Fucking Diem!"*

- Carmen Acevedo Butcher
Poet and translator of Brother Lawrence's *Practice of the Presence* (Broadleaf) and *The Cloud of Unknowing* (Shambhala)

Everything old is new again; New York is its same old self, the kids in the hallway of Ithaca High are asking the same questions, and people are learning the same astonishing lessons, realizing, "My body's all wrong for this kind of dance." This world is better taken in with your shoes off. Even if it sometimes hurts.

- J.D. Isip
Author of *Kissing the Wound* (Moontide Press) and *Pocketing Feathers* (Sadie Girl Press)

In this genre-defying hybrid collection, Lynne Kemen tests the borders between prose and poetry, between the written word and visual art. Prose poems and ekphrastic works mingle with memoir; flash fiction stands beside lineated poetry. Weaving throughout this brilliant tapestry is the story of Lucy, a barefoot heroine wandering like Wordsworth's Lucy through the "Delaware County Blue" skies of the western Catskills. Lucy grows from child to woman and finds new worlds to wander, vividly and lovingly described, but always carries with her the memory of "where little meant everything."

- Kathryn Kulpa
Author of *Cooking Tips for the Demon-Haunted* and *Girls on Film* (kathrynkulpa.com)

Lynne Kemen is a good poet, finding her own way in terms of themes and style, not looking over her shoulder at whatever may be happening in the literary bazaars. She deserves generous attention.

- John Robert Lee
Saint Lucian writer

The world Lynne Kemen writes about is the same one the rest of us inhabit. But like an Instagram filter, she applies effects atop the everyday through layers of language, rhythm, and form, her hyperfocus acting as a brake on ordinary lived experience, slowing observation down to a frame-by-frame crawl in which every detail is remarked and remembered with a limbic intensity most commonly associated with post-disaster recollections. Whether she's channeling a high school class reunion or Gogh-ing there one particular starry night, Kemen is a wise seer of the past, present, future...and, most unsettlingly, the unseen.

- Linda Lowen
Author of *Secret Syracuse* (Reedy Press) and book reviewer for a well-known publishing industry trade magazine

The beautiful stories and poems in *Shoes For Lucy* will stay on your mind. The vivid language and careful details bring them to life as if they are our own experiences. Painting with words, Lynne Kemen wears her heart on her sleeve, navigating the complexities of love, family, and memory with kindness and courage.

- Lorette C. Luzajic
founding editor, *The Ekphrastic Review*

Lynne Kemen has a keen eye for the world, but the eye of a fly with its many lenses. Connections with loss, nature, ekphrastic responses to art forms, rural life, family rifts and bonds all find home in her skilled language. Infused with a tinge of magic realism, a brief touch of the divine, *Shoes for Lucy* bears the weight of everyday emotion and familiar griefs with grace and wisdom.

- Georgia A. Popoff
Poet Laureate of Onondaga County, NY (2022-2024)

Previous Work

Grateful acknowledgment is made to the editors of the following publications for work previously published with them, sometimes in earlier versions: *Fresh Words, Honey Guide 8, Lothlorien Poetry Journal, Poetica Review, Seeing Things, Silver Birch, Spill Words, Stone Poem Quarterly, The Blue Mountain Review, The Ekphrastic Review, Topical Poetry, What We See On Our Journeys,*

Introduction

Sometimes an homage to art, jazz, or science, always an homage to memory, *Shoes for Lucy* holds the ache of loss in a family album of poetry. Looking back in the rearview mirror, the past is presented in vivid detail. From her grandmother's coat that smells of "camphor, cramped quarters, and old dreams," we're invited to visit Bisbee's General Store, to watch the Lawrence Welk Show, and to heed the advice, "Don't Postpone Joy." Though the speaker of one poem claims, "There are both older and younger ghosts. You can't see them," Lynne Kemen sees them clearly. *Shoes for Lucy* evokes a litany of memories in sepia tone, and many readers will agree, "If I remembered Gram's secret code, I could scoot back to where little meant everything."

—Ellen Bass

Ellen Bass's most recent collection, Indigo, was published by Copper Canyon Press in 2020.

for Ellen Bass

Contents

Put Your Shoes On, Lucy 1
A Stroke, But Not of Luck 2
Crows Fly at Night 3
Cows 4
Afternoon at Otego Creek 5
Bubbling 6
Three Things I Did Today 7
Conjugal Dancing 8
Game of Sorry 9
Apiary Aches 10
Persephone Ponders 11
Channeling Loss 12
Small Examination 14
Pink Reading Glasses 15
Nothing Pointy 16
After Jean, 1932 17
Saudade, et tu? 18
AWP Seattle 2023 19
Dear Lord, It's Loud 20
Bisbee's 21
Last Wound-up 22
Barn's Burnt Down 23
Like a Sycamore 24
Sordid Heap 25
Keep Your Hands Off 26
Cinnamon Toast, Winter 1954 27
The Discount 28
Blue Deer 29
Empress of the Blues 30
Nana's Plush Coat 31
Say It 32
Moss Haiku 33
As It Happens 34
What You've Heard Is True 35
Meridale Clocks 36
The Kitchen Remembers My World 37
Ana One, Ana Two 38
By the Time We Arrived 39
Dab of Blue 40
Dancing in Seville 41
Lazy Afternoon 42
The Fall of Icarus 43

Icicles	44
Beth	45
Ode to My Father	46
A Found Poem	48
Dragon of a Plantation	49
For the Sake of My Children	50
Nonchalantly	51
That One Last Wild Summer	52
Breaking Free of Mary Oliver	53
Ghosts Don't Know Joy or Remember Symbols	54
The War of Happening	55
Treadwell	56
Cloud Studies 1&2	58
Mrs. Potato Head	59
Nebra Sky Disc	61
Moving	62
ISCCP Conference	63
Living Room	64
Nuns in an Egg	65
Staring at Stars	66
Merce Cunningham	67
Somene's Been Here	68
I Prefer	69
Dimming Day	70
Non-Objective Composition, Flight of an Airplane	71
Night Light Garish, 1978	72
Sunflower, Sunshine, Sun	73
Maud	74
NY Movie, Edward Hopper 1939	75
Piet Mondrian's Name is an Anagram	76
Ithaca High School, class of 1969	77
Falling Off a Log	78
Yankee Poem	80

More Than a Handful

Returning 82
Gazing 84
The Creek 85
The Path 86
Big Baby Dowl 87
The Turtle 88
The Circus 89
Mum and Bernie's House, Meridale 1960 90
Out in the Raised Beds 91
Three Easy Pieces 92
Beside the Night Stand 93
Deer in the Drive 94
Origami 95
And When It's Over 96
Three More Haiku 97
The Best Advice 98

Acknowledgments 99

Put Your Shoes On, Lucy

"Put Your Shoes On, Lucy," Lucy Finch's mother said when it was time to go. Lucy preferred barefoot. Shoes came off at home or Nana and Poppy's house. Nana fussed about the cold floors in winter, 72 degrees plenty warm. Floors carpeted except kitchens, bathrooms, Poppy's grass incredibly soft. Lucy loved the feel of blades on toes.

Shoes stayed on at Grandma and Grandpa's. So cold in the house, windows bore rime, and anything too far from the fireplace or wood-burning stove froze. Water from the tap so cold it was slushy. Lucy drank many glasses, even though her teeth ached. Always ginger molasses or shortbread cookies to eat with that font of water.

Mom said it to people wearing shoes, like her father. And when it was time to wave goodbye said, "Write if you get work," and someone else said "Hang by your thumbs". Lots seemed silly to Lucy. Grownups always laughed, but never told her why it was funny.

Visits to both grandparents became weekly after they moved to Ithaca. Grandma and Grandpa celebrated golden anniversary, big party, cake. Grandpa stayed in his study.

He'd appear, glare, retreat. Lucy and five of her six cousins outside, waded in creek, raced pieces of wood. Baby stayed in a bassinet. People said "too bad grandpa's forgetful", hardening arteries - the party went on. Grandma enjoyed the celebration anyway. Grandma's church friends dropped by. June day and sky was what Lucy called "Delaware County Blue". A stark contrast to Ithaca's frequent overcast.

Lucy's uncle showed movies of everyone on a portable screen. Its surface felt like sandpaper, but sparkly white. Touching it, the screen, Mother said better not, it hurts sometimes.

A Stroke, But Not of Luck

A man once cared for his demented wife. Blinding pain, put his hands to his face, and then saw confusion. To the caretaker he asked, *Are these mine?*

Watching *Dancing with The Stars,* the caretaker was in a ballgown; he was in a tuxedo. She curtsied deeply and then she called the man's daughter and told the child to come. The man's daughter took all of the money in her house and sped towards her father on the wings of an owl. The winds were blowing fiercely against their direction, the owl was ruffled. He stopped for potato chips.

Mad with grief, full of exhaustion from caring for his wife, she was shriveled. An aged princess, in a magic spell of confusion and distance. She shirked his kisses, wouldn't hold his hand. He saw her but sat with a ghost who was awake all night, who hissed, and shouted, and blamed him. Baba Yaga, her legs were scrawny, with claws, a wicked tongue.

The daughter didn't believe Daddy could die. She held his hand, and she couldn't stand, and it was cold. Always, six feet apart, now six feet below.

Don't go. Don't go. After no answer, *It's alright, then, you can go. I'm here. I will carry on.* And just like that, Death sat back. Black blood ran out of his mouth. Was it his brain? Was it his soul? The daughter didn't ever know.

A man in shorts and a t-shirt ran into the room. *Hi, he had a massive ICH, it tore through the right occipital. Want to see the scan?*

At the man's home, the caretaker had changed into Peter Rabbit's mother. The man's wife was watching, head cocked, questioning.

-*Mom, it will be all right.*
-*No, it won't.*
And she was right.

Crows Fly at Night

Five tribes of Kulin Nation say
we crows fly home at night,
finding our own kind.

Noongar aboriginals say
we carry their dead across
to Kurannup.

In this Nation,
a flock is a murderous gang.
A murder is better than being alone.

Smart, tool makers
talking in caws,
we frighten the superstitious,
scared of shadows and disease.

Bees dance, waggle, telling their tribe
where to find the sweetest clover.

We sit on telephone wire
without shade,
a threat to gardens.
Scared off by our own corpses.
We won't be back.

If I weren't left without wings
I'd fly at night.
I'd fly home to my tribe.
Never. Ever. Alone.

Cows

The cows, loose, standing, in my neighbor's field.
I groan, bushwhacked,
that field for my neighbor.
He comes home this weekend.

Honey, call Marilyn. Her cows are loose.
I trudge to the cows with a white pail, empty,
they don't know that.

Marilyn arrives beside Bob.
Where are the calves?
I see no calves. Just cows.
Wait. These aren't our cows.
Whose then?

They've gotta be Cubbie's.
He's in town, says he'll be back soon.
But shit. They aren't his.

My day evaporates. Who the hell
might be missing cows? Ruth:
*We sold ours out in the spring. But Wilber uses
our fields to keep his cows. I'll call him.*

Finally, Wilbur wanders up to claim his cows.
A white pail, some grain, the cows go slowly home,
across my neighbor's land.

Afternoon at Otego Creek

Water's whisper echoes
sun through leaves.
Shouts sling out
an August afternoon.

Sun through leaves.
In the stream, flotsam floats.
Across an August afternoon,
feet dance.

Quit it! I mean it!
Feet dance.
Voices silenced.

Quit it! I mean it!
Shots snap out.
Voices silenced.
Waters whisper echoes.

Bubbling

Swirling steaminess. Boys gather round. Silence — crickets. Too shy to do more than stare. Enough to knock you off your bike.

Seasonal autumnal weather, but forever summer for these guys. Doused in Brill cream, a little dab'll do ya. Freezing look of model, *Don't even try to approach or touch.* But she knows that she is searing into brains beyond this moment.

Impulsivity until twenty-five. Life in a bubble, both, no all. It's all airbrushed.

Three Things I Did Today

In the morning, hand outstretched,
calling brave black-capped chickadees,
neighborly nuthatches, tiny titmice.
Feathers fan around us as
we talk, trading thoughts.

I climb into paintings
to pace the fearful frame,
wickedly in suspension.
Everything is exhausting.
Breaking to understand, bending to
to get in, to get out,
to come home.

From bed, I beg for Beethoven,
big surges of
not platonic
pillow talk.

But his piano fashions peace,
and plays me to sleep.

The sweet keys keep me,
snuggled symphonically for six months,
I become the I am *I am* with him.

Conjugal Dancing

I dance, you dance, he dances, she dances, you dance.
It all looks simple, I conjugate it,
conjugal dancing– almost.
The figures aren't stiff, but supple.
Salsa, bachata, merengue, switch weight, left to the
right, sensual. Roll those hips. Hear
the persistent beat.

The skin is uniform. I change it up to reflect the blue
sheen. Primary, primal. A turning point of my painting.
I went to school until third grade.
My paintings are first grade, couldn't sell them. My characters
are life when I write poetry.

Conjugate it. I dance, you dance, he dances, you dance,
we dance.
Life is often hard, harder to let go.

Game of Sorry

Summer at the cabin,
Grace cantilevered, a human bridge.
String beans, growth spurts.
Under quartz light, porch light,
a fizz of Welch's grape soda.

Quiet moment. Shouting later.
Rose's building tired,
hungry, the inner need to go to
sleep.

Blue and white checked tablecloth
covered with books, glasses, ashtray.
Rose's shock at losing Sorry.
It's not fair!

Apiary Aches

Bees love catnip; they go crazy for it; afterward, we drowsed, full of honeyed sweetness like the bees that browse the catnip, it could be like catnip to us, and I remember the first time my Siamese kitten had catnip, how she crawled into the bathtub and yowled in such a way that we were never sure if she liked it or not, but later she tried it again and

was blissfully sprawled on her back, belly exposed — it can be like that sometimes, you're never sure if the first time is *godawful* or good as Motown, all that nasty, dirty shit, but they say it with panache, so we buzz along, undisturbed.

Coldness produces boldness as we pause, immobile, frozen by frost, beating our wings harder to motion back dead/undead but never resurrected warmth returned and wing torn struggling so hard. I wonder if bees sting each other the way we did, if it hurts so much for them as it does for us. Do bees part, pollen left behind, join another swarm, not so humble, fuzzy heads turned away, as we do when we do come to the same flower,

Persephone Ponders

Persephone peers out without blinking. Six months marred by darkness; three years locked down. Time unkindly tick-tocks differently in all the halls of Hades. Flickers of sinister snickering, the recognition of blossoming, of leafing. The corpse, a contrast, half-seen in rings on Zoom.

On smart screens always seen binge-watching on-demand on sea and on land.

And Persephone? Her fleeting youth yearns to share food off another's plate. To share a sip of wine — touch lips in between. But Winter is harsh. It's complicated. Unnecessary stupidity may be muted, taken off video, she leaves, leaving an avatar to suffer in her place.

It's torturous and tremulous, to listen, to endure unenticing voices.

You: *Pssst...come out, don't stay, let's play. Embrace me, running free, to sway the moon together, and dance.*

Come out, uncloak and unmask, no longer the chained task of Hades.

Soft spring brings relief. Winter whipped by warmer weather, your lips pressed against new limbs. Suck the soma from those buds and smash nothing.

And Hades? He's sitting in solitude, unloved and unpitied.

Persephone proceeds with levity. She skirts the scars of drama, ecstatically donning fuzzy socks, no leather skirts, just jammies. Netflix and chill suspended 'til next spring, making the best of hell.

Channeling Loss

-for Liz Huntington

Smiling, dreaming, reaching
for someone I need
to survive loss - you.
It is *you*.

There. But not there - you.
So frustrating. Just when I need
you most. When I want *us*. Stifling
silence sits.

I'm here. You are wherever
and everywhere. I find reminders
of you daily. Bookmarked
books, notebooks, jotted notes,
groceries, ideas for a class. No longer
needed pills. Can't throw it away, toss
it out; it's just junk. *Precious*.

This house won't let me leave.
Cursed by your clothes.
Fading - time - fleeting brutal
truth each return.
Every - damned - time.

Every memory
wrapped, unwrapped,
rewrapped, swaddled.
Don't make maudlin from change.
There's only anger and ache.

Outside, fresh air.
Walk, move. Gotta move.
Don't look down. Don't
stop moving. I mustn't. I mustn't.
This is my time.
This is my step.

We stepped in time.
You.

A pair of old shoes
Under the couch-*you*.
Worn down. Just toss 'em,
I told you, but now I see.
I see.

Small Examination

Listen to the rain on a tin roof.
Drops dance, drum their tiny feet.
Thunder growls, drops dribble.

Listen to the trees battle for their lives,
leaves and branches bristling,
bark banged up, bruised.

Occasionally feathers fly solo,
chased by clouds, plumage,
bedraggled, dragged through mud.

Listen to tires on the county road, rutted
pavement cracked, Queen Anne's Lace
un-tatted, unloved by the shoulders.

It is raining here-autumn pushes
apples away, lets them drop
careless, unheeding.

Pink Reading Glasses

Poppy's reading glasses were pink before pink was cool.
They often sat on his head instead of on his broken nose.
Look, it's broken! No cartilage! As he smeared it sideways.
Left, right, right back to left. Mine murmured *no*,
refused to roll.

Sun glinted off the glasses,
smiled.

Blue eyes became huge
behind the pink glasses.
I tried them, dizzy,
dancing while magnified.

Poppy protected peonies,
rooted roses, mixed mulch,
recorded his grass mixtures:
Zoysia, Fine Fescue, St. Augustine.
My eyes rolled as he extolled,
but I do remember the sun shining.
I'm still running across his lawn.

Softest blades ever, like butter,
greenest grass living large in
a tiny world of fertilizers,
twiddled turf formulas.

Nothing Pointy

Burnt orange background for warmth
roundness, spirals, buttery pinwheels-
nothing pointy or masculine.
Seashells, wombs,
easter eggs in a basket

Comets cartwheeling, planets spinning
You are here.
Rolling baked rolls with cinnamon-
spirals, round, soft
tops, toys, skeins of yarn, tails trailing.

Roundness reaching into hugs,
sweet embrace, delicate writing
loopily scrawled,
no signature, *you know it's me.*

After Jean, 1932

Months after Jean died of pneumonia at 14,
just before penicillin. Remaining family
in front of my great aunt's home.

Grandmother clutches her pocketbook.
Grandfather clutches his hands behind his back.
He never touches anyone.

A soldier stands at ease with no ease.
At nine, Uncle Jim stares bravely. Soon he enlists
in the war.

Mother stands next to Jim. She's
shocked, her universe slammed shut with Jean.
Her father, closed in his study, only comes out to eat.

Her father, the Town Supervisor,
delivers the graduation
speech for ninth graders.

An empty chair is there where his oldest favorite
should be. Jean isn't seen. He still gives
her speech. The church doesn't catch him again until
he is in his casket.

Saudade, et tu?

I miss getting together for Christmas.
Well, I miss getting together.
Perhaps next year.
But we both know
a bad case of Saudade,
of spilled milk, something souring.
Too many tongues bitten,
too many words that wound
too much pent-up, unwound.
We stand by the winter pond,
Look each other in the eye,
Then look away.
That dead fish look,
frozen in time.

AWP, Seattle 2023
American Writers and Poets Conference

Already arriving,
heading for their hotels.
They were looking for friends,
enemies, frenemies, anyone.
They checked in, peered
down corridors, checked out elevators,
texted those at home, "Finally here".
They met friends, FB friends, zoom friends.
They shared self-conscious hugs.
It wasn't familiar being with so many.
They brought books.
They brought fears.
They brought unrealistic hopes.
They went to the bar. They couldn't drink. They drank too much.
They went outside, shared a joint.
There was –was that whatshername? Whoosits?
How could they catch their breath?
How could they stop trembling?
How did everyone else seem so confident?
Arrogant bastards!
They went to panels.
They went to parties.
They went to readings by angry people.
There were readings by sad people.
They wished they were home.
They watched the famous.
They dreamed of success.
They shared stories, gossip, contract details.
They were exhausted.
Finally, they were departing.
All flights cancelled for twenty-four hours.
Hold me, pick me up, take me home.

Dear Lord, It's Loud

Cacophony of china,
the clatter. Voices high.

Old oil smoke
co-mingling and creating sensory
chaos. In lunch hour heat,
there are too many sweaty men.

The ceiling fan fails to keep up
with unpleasant heat,
kitchen heat, summer heat,
street heat.

Mechanics on two-hour lunches,
unconcerned, laughing. Dear Lord, it's loud,
then dwindles down,
not in a hurry.

Washing dishes, leftovers
tossed in the trash.
Worn-out waitresses sigh
beside cooks, preparing.

Bisbee's

The sign said, *E.S. Bisbee, general store*. Also Post Office. A flag flung, one person always leaning on the railing. Everett or Burt were fixtures.

The glass said *groceries*; it was mostly canned goods, dry goods, rubber boots and car parts. And candy! Bubblegum cigars, red lips, wax mustaches, penny candy and a long low freezer with popsicles.

Competing smells made me giddy: cheddar cheese wheels, salami, ham with pink and green-colored chunks, potatoes that still smelled of earth. Apples or peaches piled next to animal cages and feed.

Gasoline and kerosine mixed with the scent of wooden floorboards.

The Post Office had little boxes you could peer into. Doors with brass filigree, a knob with numbers, the secret code. Gram let me open it while she traded. Once the door opened, a "post-officy" smell of paper and glue.

The heart of the community, Bisbee's, stood until April of 1976. The furnace failed, and the whole place flamed into a funeral pyre. Ruez Bisbee was in his 70s then, too. Too tired and too heartbroken for his melted antique cash register.

If I remembered Gram's secret code, I could scoot back to where little meant everything.

Last Wound-Up

The Last Wound-Up
Columbus Avenue
New York City
Windup firetrucks, sushi-spinning.
Nathan owned the joint
crusty, crinkly, cognizant,
a crowd of toys around him.

His store's sign said
"Don't Postpone Joy"—
Just call to the cosmos
Carpe Fucking Diem!
I didn't listen.
Arrogance leaves a stubborn
scent.

Long gone, the store's corpse
I still visit. The store now a cemetery
of dreams.
Nathan nagging me, like a
damned ghost of Dickens—
Don't Postpone Joy

.

Barn's Burnt Down

Barn's burnt down and now I can see the moon
- Mizuta Masahide (17th-century Japanese poet and samurai)

Imagine you live your vision.
You jump at a half-dreamt idea.
It now deals you.

Barn's burnt down.
Owls hide from the moon.
Birds burnt amongst all your things:
photos, paintings, books.

Not freeing as
I thought.
Firemen sift through ashes and
that terrible smell.

Wiping fallen tears,
a cross of ash across
your forehead.

Like a Sycamore

They all had a reason.
Excuses or lists of why.
Butterscotch balls mouthed,
clicking against their teeth,
tangled against their lying tongues.
Like a sycamore,
the roundness of honed hip-hop,
singing their internal songs.
Some sang a song of exasperation,
deliberately sang sotto voce,
but various words sprang out
in clumps, like a sycamore.
Give it to Jesus. I don't care.
Humming like the rattling blossom
of a sycamore. You call it
an English Elm but it was just
a sycamore.
Common, stolid, deep roots
staunchly grounded.
I grind my teeth, too exasperated
to listen—
words rustling in the wind.

Sordid Heap
After "Anti-Poetica" by Danez Smith

Who cares concerning
wasted time?
Curled into wretched ways,
fingernails raw-rimmed.
Eyes hooded, swollen, unfocused.

Incompetent.
Pear-shaped bruises
under my eyes.

Fanatical roving eyes
unfocused only to
see shit. *This shit.*

Found unresponsive,
don't seek out my sister.
She's an icy one, wrapped in a
normal life.

Like Billy Holiday*: Don't explain!*
Trust your reader.
Hate yourself.

Keep Your Hands Off

When I was five, we moved in with my grandmother. My father was traveling, and we needed to save money. Mom got her old room. I got the dressing room. It wasn't even a room. No door, just a dark green curtain that sometimes moved by itself. Grandmother called it the sewing room, but no one ever sewed there. There were some racks of clothes. It all smelled of grandmother's old perfume, and dust.

At night, headlights from slow-moving cars sent shadows walking up the walls. I knew that they were watching, waiting to grab me. I kept my eyes shut tight. I could hear them breathing. There was a wooden and metal plaque on the wall. During the day, it looked okay, but at night it turned into a wolf, and I was afraid to get up to go to the bathroom. I tried not to look at it. Sometimes I wet the bed instead of getting caught by the shadows.

Once, on a weekend visit, Dad tried to show me that there was nothing there. He brought a big flashlight, but I couldn't bear to look. He grumbled and said living with women made me "sensitive."

There was a little girl who lived next door: Cathy. My mother called her Chatty Cathy and said she looked like a doll. We used to play together until Grandmother said she didn't entertain people from the village. After that, I played alone.

While cleaning up Mom's place, I found a photo of Cathy and me. The back of the picture said *Sam and Cathy, 1959*. My face was blurred. Cathy did look like a doll. Behind us, pressed against the glass door, horrible hands.

I'm a grandfather now; time, not fear, crawls up my spine. What hands? What did they want, reaching out? Dead people whisper in that sewing room and breathe under the bed in the dark.

Cinnamon Toast, Winter 1954

-For Norma Howard

Norma made cinnamon toast.
It was my first ever taste of that treat.
I sat in the wooden chair, at the kitchen table.

It was a blend of familiar and not.
Same toast but with a different look!
The toast was cut diagonally
and it had a mixture of sugar and cinnamon
sprinkled on top.

Warm, buttery, sparkly, cinnamon that
tasted a little like chewing on the red
and blue wooden sticks of my tinker toys.
Woody, with a Christmas cookie sparkle
and slightly bitter taste.

Reddish-brown like the crayon my Dad called brick.
It didn't taste like the crayon. The sugar got on my face,
it stung when Norma brushed it off.

There was a glass of milk to go with it.
The milk was cold and felt good with the toast.
I blew bubbles in the milk and Norma laughed
instead of getting mad at me.

The Discount

Something inside likes a discount.

The moon comes over thrilling mountains,
and you are unsure if you are getting a real deal or being bilked.

You bite the metal to be sure it is genuine,
and you feel only the thrill of the sale,
Does it come in blue?

Blue Deer

- *for Sondra Freckelton*

A blue deer brings her baby.
A bestial bouquet on a blue day.
The third anniversary from the death of another,
gratitude, verisimilitude empties.
New life never fills that void.

We meet in woods, no longer wary.
I hum or sing, deer and woodland fairy,
of animals who soothe or intrinsically fit
the morning.

You meander with a leggy fawn
free of fear; the deers' tails wag.
We want to touch but don't. We
meet and greet. You smile with your
child.

I christen the baby in her name, Freckelton.
Part of the humor will undoubtedly fade,
indelibly indigo inked on my heart.

Empress of the Blues

Bessie, regal, roosting,
smoldering, sensual
number bouquet,
flowers

canary overhead, febreezy flaunting
sixteen-piece band belonging only to
Bessie

plutocratic notes-richness
tabloids, street smack
anagram of cinema iceman desire

Nana's Plush Coat

The plush coat, labeled: Marshall Fields, Chicago.
The black a bruised purplish-red,
belonging to my grandmother.

An expensive coat -
once, packed away in the attic
for 50 years in slumber and finally given to me;
it smelled of camphor, cramped quarters,
and old dreams.
Nana was a flapper...
...or a flapper as much as farm life allowed
in Nebraska.

Nana
worried that I would
take all of what she called LDS. She, we, wouldn't
talk about war.
Or sex,
but she still gave me her coat. She trusted
me.

I wore the coat to death -in college-
Anti-war rallies, to meetings
about Buddhism and B'hai,
Bob Dylan concerts,
The Dead One More Saturday Nighting.
Clapton in Cream, a drunken frat boy spilled beer on me
in Barton Hall. Or was it Cambridge, or Boston, or Storrs,
or Ithaca. No matter.
In it I felt elegant.

Say It

I tuck my neurodiversity in my pocket,
free of adversity.
It's the right thing to do,
isn't it? Isn't it? Isn't it?

I play words. Some wonderful
to say, to say, to say.
Sometimes they make sounds.

I can't stand to say *Sheila*. Or *Wanda*.
I hate what it does to
my mouth,
so I don't say it.
Never, never, never.
Ever.

Moss Haiku

moss on my stone step
not so many visitors
I feel quite alone

moss for trees and shrubs
railroad diorama scene
bryophyte for play

clever gardeners know
moss and lichen not the same
they grow on me

As It Happens

As it happens, reeling
from losses of strangers,
Joan Didion always slouched.
She made it glamorous,
articulate, and suave.

As it happens, Desmond Tutu
said "You don't choose your family.
They are God's gift to you, as you are
to them."
He sat beside the Dali Lama.

They are the largest
family.

"We should preserve every scrap
of biodiversity as priceless while we learn
to use it and come to understand
what it means to humanity."
As it happens, EO Wilson was able
to understand the communication
between ants. He never invited me
to call him Ed, but I secretly did.

What You've Heard Is True

What you've heard is true. All of it. It's about Leahy Lane. My grandfather told me that he saw it with his own two eyes. Doc Orrin Leahy, for whom the lane was named, was a veterinarian who was fetched to the area farms with a two-wheeled gig, always whistling along the way. Doc's hands were huge and always red, but he was gentle with animals.

A dairy community, Franklin was a no-lace dress world. Many racked to ruin trying to make ends meet. If they couldn't pay Doc for work with money, they paid him with eggs, bread, or honey.

Young people would drive down and halt at the good doctor's farm. In the trees and on poles hung skeletons, skulls, and noisemakers. When the wind blew, they all made strange and eerie sounds. The medicine house nearby contained bottles and jars of every size and description. Everything from skunk oil to a human fetus was pickled in a special preservative. Maurice Huddleston bought the farm in 1922, Grandpa said the girlfriends moved closer to their beaus when they wandered through this weird place.

Perhaps strangest of all was a human skeleton hanging by his feet. Head heading downward. Somehow, Doc had strung him together, and his bones knocked together in the wind. No one seemed to know about a missing body, but there he was. He was dressed in old-fashioned clothing. Doc once told Frank Gibson that there was no cause to be afraid. The Hanging Man made Doc think of our ultimate surrender, sacrifice, or being suspended in time.

Meridale Clocks

Lucy's first memory of her grandparent's house is the hell between three windup clocks. None in synch, tick-tocks, each bong or chime, rings alone.

The kitchen clock is her favorite.
Eldest, small, no frills.

The main room (dining/living/family room), on the mantle two clocks, both weekly windups. Tall, spare, rectangular, with a painted glass front.

Her sister is feminine, with delicately etched glass. She lives on the sideboard in Lucy's dining room, within speaking distance of each other, Lucy doesn't wind either. She knows they whisper the passing of time.

Lucy and Benjamin lived in Manhattan for 34 years, across from Lincoln Center, but came to their upstate farmhouse to live full-time six years ago.

Choosing the farmhouse for them, not so different from their first home. There's a woman in a rich brown dress who also lives here. She silently winds them, cares for them, marks time with them. Lucy doesn't mention the woman to anyone except Benjamin.

Once, she told a friend that she thought that Nana haunted her former home and later was asked about it by someone she'd never met. Small towns, loose tongues. Lucy doesn't want to share the woman with strangers.

She's happy that the clocks are back where they came from.

The Kitchen Remembers My World

Muted, barren interior. Starkly
aching to color it.
Death does away with worry.

Who will starve my sunflower?
Forsaken, who carries
it home?

"For Sale" signs that my
neighbors are gone. Odd, old
couple. He, long-bearded,
she shuffles, disheveled.

Screen door jams, it dampens
my mood. Clinging, the kitchen
remembers my world
in black and white,
damn the color.

Ana One, Ana Two

After your mother's descent into Alzheimer's, you visit her every weekend. Early Friday mornings you board the bus from New York City to Binghamton, transfer to Ithaca. Then you reverse the trip on Sunday. On a bus every weekend.

Every morning, at 7:30, you teach and advise students until 8 PM. Then you go home. Your husband calls from work or emails to check in. Dinner is thrown together. Then to bed. In the middle of the night you get up and watch the George Washington Bridge twinkling lights until morning.

Your friends drop by to ask you to lunch. You say *Perhaps another time*. You try to get work done. Mostly you sit in your office and stare out the window at Park Avenue. You cry at inopportune times.

Weekends, you try to give your father a break from caretaking. He resists going to bed, stays up, and falls asleep in his chair. You sit next to your mother. to her hospital-style bed, and rock in the rocker. It's not as obvious that you are rocking that way.

Your mother does not sleep at night. Sometimes she is lost and scared, repeating, "Can someone please help me?"

You watch Lawrence Welk with her.

Your mother loves this program. She watches the show the way your goddaughter watched Teletubbies. It's all wunnerful. The Lennon Sisters are still girls. The lovely Norma Zimmer, Champaign Lady. The goddamn bubble machine. Myron Floren playing accordion. They are all so clean, so not sexy. And Lawrence Welk calls them his family. You have no family, just two broken parents.

The dog lies at your feet, thumping her tail, almost in time to the music.

By the Time We Arrived

It was snowing hard.
We shucked coats, boots, scarves,
moved toward the fireplace.
Too hot in the room, damn hot.
My contact lenses stuck from the creosote in the air.
Ruby sat in her seat, bundled in two bulky sweaters,
and a turtleneck, the chair conformed to her body.

I introduced my friend Cheryl to her.
Ruby stared, as country people often do. No smile.
I was sharing two friends from two parts of my life.

Cheryl seemed self-conscious, too. She mentioned Yale and
Stanford in the first ten minutes.
Ruby thought that she meant Stamford New York, and
asked, did she know Burton Wheeler.
Cheryl did not.

Dab of Blue

De Stijl, be still, the universe! Stare at lines. Horizontal and vertical only- *so strict*. Let's look inside. Dab of blue, the only relief.

Look at that blue, all that white space. The architectural grid for growing gardens. Some gaze inward without outward distractions. Black lines keep
us in line.

Like the formal maze gardens or the sand sculpture,
any awareness wakes.

Dancing in Seville

It's hot, but everyone continues to dance. It's a confection of skirts. Sweet apples, bananas.
Snapping, swishing, twirling fabric. Feet landing hard. It's impossible to ignore. It's contagious. Everyone is dancing. Around the corner, there is laughter, gossip. It is delicious to forget about fears.

Tia Dolores is dancing with a chair. She thumps it in time to the music, dares anyone to challenge her choice of partner.

The men are sitting this one out. Women slip their arms through each other's. It's thirsty work dancing. There is perspiration mingled with perfume, a fine stink. Tomorrow, there will be aching heads, sore legs, body aches. But today it doesn't matter.

Lazy Afternoon
After Pete La Roca

Late lazy morning,
not quite afternoon,
Pete La Roca rocks the room.
Then, with percussion, sin, and
two Steves: Swallow and Kahn.
together, they went beyond Hitchcockian harmony.
It's shadow play.

Sit down, meditate, focus on the fuller
brush man, a touch so light it feels transparent.
La Roca has no heavy hand, he scat sings in
your head, in your ear, tickles memories
of dreams, it's raining blues. Drops, steady,
subtle. Before you know it, you are
hypnotized by brushy sounds. Like watching
snowflakes melt on the windshield. Synesthesia
blues, floating. A 1930s film noir, full of shadows.

Henderson hocks his soul slowly.
The Rock truly and surly,
Such sticks.
Soft, what light through
yonder touch barely breaks.
These musicians undertake the work
to make it work. Buddies becoming
breath, to riff in rhythm.

The want to whisper,
Fingers blistered rich and rewarding.
New York Times and snow,
rough cut sugar cubes, men cut from jazz
and the blues-heavy rain.

The Fall of Icarus

His foreground almost overlooked.
Peasant in bright orange, stares at the ground. The shepherd
stares skyward. Both see nothing.

It's funny, how the focus isn't Icarus.
How eponymous is an afterthought.
An epic accident off-center,
a flailing leg, featherless,
plucked from the sky.

A serene sea, Ships serenely sail.
Sail on.
I don't wanna know
where you're going.

Bruegel's choices of Suffield
Green, Clunch, Smoked Trout, Cola channeling
Farrow & Ball in the twenty-first century.

Lulled, we are culled into doldrums.
No transcendental *transit*.
Ob-la-di Ob-la-da.
Life goes on.

Icicles

On a Sunday,
March
Icicles
glinting,
sun
spilling,
drilling
into my
naked
eyes.

Tree
encircled
in ice,
drips
leaking light.
Rivulets
the wind
puts in
place.

Icy stream
stops,
half-frozen.
Last year's leaves still scattered.

Beth

Everyone else thinks my mom is sweet.
Mother doesn't smile at me.
No one wrestled with her rages.

I did, and I do
hear how a mother killed her kid.
Imagine a mother maiming,
much less murdering.
She could. She can.

A young woman in college
while World War II waged,
Betty became Beth, a different time,
a changed person.

The war pounded out. Men came home.
Women again mothers without work.
No princess, she was pissed.
Many mothers couldn't mend.
It still stands undiscussed.

Mother meant to be a doctor.
This kid nixed even that idea.

Father found a career. Away four nights a week.
Mother maudlin at home with me.
She, always irritated. Me, with frequent earaches.

Often, to her, too much.
She bolted my bedroom door from the outside.
She banished me behind the bolt.
Out of the eye of the storm,
Mother calmed.

My body ended any idea I'd mother.
Vacant, I gaped when Mother asked
for grandchildren.

Ode to My Father

A smart ass. Too smart,
he skipped two grades and stepped into
Cornell at 16. Six years of vet school in three.

He still earned wages at Egan's meat market,
drinking deep at The Palms.

He bought me Lincoln Logs
and New American Plastic Bricks-
for *him* to play with.
He built homes and doll beds, too,
for my Ginny Dolls,
and fuzzy kittens.

Son- of-a -bitch.
Daddy!
Don't tell your mother.
Forbidden words constructed.
The air, blue.

Words to popular songs poorly kept:
"Wake Up Little Susie", "The Wabash Cannonball".
"And you can tell your friend there with you, he'll have to go".

He fed our boxer beer.
Radio never exactly found a station
we could clearly hear.
13 broken coffee pots in the cellar he swore
he'd fix.

Often gone to dead-stop disease.
Not all were pleased.
A farmer met him in the drive with a shotgun.
Harsh words for a Government Man,
but Daddy talked him down.
The stranger shouldered his
shot gun and they soon began
to be friends.

Coffee, Lucky Strikes, beer, martinis.
Pacing-always.

Preferred the barber and the gravedigger to
academics. Earned several degrees
with no degrees of patience for those who
wore theirs with pride.

He never bought into any of my boyfriends,
They all want the same thing.

-Listen, Missy, it's my way or the highway, by God.
-No sassing.
-One of us is going to end up crying.

He broke my nose.
Wrecked my nose with his wedding ring.
Six months of nosebleeds.
Maslow's Heirarchy of Needs–
an apology.
Not one word said.
Wound never healed.
We, both violently stubborn.

Too young for WWII,
too old for Korea.
Viet Nam parted us.
But war sat well with him.

Then Kent State happened.
Home for the weekend,
his world shaken. His words weak.
Shocked, he could barely speak.
They shot kids!

I graduated, got into grad school,
and a home out of wedlock.
Daddy abandoned me for years.
Absent at my wedding, my mother
cried, but stayed by his side.
Some wounds never heal.

He, the complicated cause of me.
Never, ever easy.
Too similar or simply opposites.

A Found Poem

I found a poem in a book about biostatistics.
Not really in but tucked into the pages. Handwritten
words on blue-lined paper, delivered or mistakenly
left. Now, un-shelved, like the book.

*This is just to say/that I love you in so many ways/
That love is part of my central tendency/tender kisses
to your extremities/dispersion to the interquartile/
parts of my heart /You might inferentially assume/
adjusting or controlling for a variable-/except it is
invariable that love and passion/it o(beyes)rules/
I have a deep, statistical bias for your lips/*

I left them to it, smoothed my chignon,
adjusted my cardigan, wiped my glasses,
and cleared my throat.

I didn't want to intrude, so turned away,
busied myself straightening books,
returned to the present.

Dragon of a Plantation

I start to think you stink
like Beowulf.
Strong, spattered with sugar or salt or death.
The fault of your lust and disgust for even the
accolade of king -
climate change indeed,
clambered, *clamored,* and enamored you
to no one.

I dreamt we hoped then saw no hope - no feet
attached to spindly old-man legs.
Can't fly away, can't take none of it for granted.
But you planted your bastard son, the gold
dragon of a plantation.

I decide desire, destiny drawings dropped
kiss, soft as a feathered angel's wings a' flutter.
Brave, guarded, glance, grin.
I wish we'd died,
grinning sightless eyes.

Be it Beowulf or Grendel, Anglo-Saxon drawn
disassembled. Anaphora resolution,
resolute. A disgusting hero's revolution.

It is a bird.

It is a man.

Norman warrior or
warbler.

For the Sake of My Children

Ripped from our land,
veins and arteries exposed.
My man must remain,
defend the homeland.

There's a hole in my heart,
organs excised.

For the sake of my children, I go.
Cranes come, settle, comfort and
protect us from dangerous snakes.

Clouds of blue and yellow
remind us of our home.
It's not all roses.
We *will* remember.

Nonchalantly

Stocking feet nonchalantly stood on
well-made centuries.
No celery greens, instead–
varied blues, reds, yellows
in patterns that start strong,
then stumble,
fall apart in a
thicket of colors.

Imagine ears listening to clicks,
clique clinks as artists laid down,
lickety-split on faux mosque floors.

That One Last Wild Summer

A cowboy's
careless, dangerous,
ice-cutting gaze.

Cigarettes. Jack Daniels.
Disturbing, alluring.
Swerving, smoking.

Faded. A photo
of his Mama
in his boot.

I am *not*
convinced.
Cornell, Ph.D. Theatre.
A ten-year plan.

Decades later, I think
of him (gratitude), a
grueling danger,
but he's mine.
That one, last, wild summer.

Breaking Free of Mary Oliver

Tell me, what is it you plan to do
with your one wild and precious life? – Mary Oliver

A challenge. A contest.
I know there's only one,
it aches me to wanna to take a nap.
To perfect the headstand I have
been working on for 10 frigg'n years.

The kitchen timer ticks loudly.
It never rings.
Sometimes I want *that*.

An onslaught of submissions.
So many rejections.
So little time.

Mary chides me.
I would burn to a cinder
to spend an hour with her.
I adore her! But what if
she's an ass? What if she
smelled of cigarettes and snitty-ness?

It's not so wild, as most lives go,
but it's mine, and I am so…

Ghosts Don't Know Joy or Remember Symbols

Séance art, frenzied, a medium
scrawls, an encounter—
an unexpected Ouija board.

Georgiana didn't wanna at first.
Born in a quiet room, but not
one minute reticent. Her guide
Larry guided her and she got it.
Complex skeins of thread across
the canvas thrown. The canvas cast,
catching, conscious/unconscious.

Spirits lack reaction. The dead
never seek expression. Messages
delivered. The living lost in
their soothing supplication. Silly
and muted, wanting a word with
the wordless.

Ghosts don't know joy or
remember symbols. She didn't
flaunt her skills. It wasn't a thrill.

The War of Happening

Stories stored,
ammunition used against
expected assailants.

A double agent
its ovum overthinking,
knowing incarceration
more innately
than a five-inch incision.

If I start, I won't stop.
Just stop.
Singe my tongue.

No survivors
on any day.
Leave. Starting over?
Or holding ground?
Ride your horses or
burn it to the ground.

Treadwell

Except for the gently rolling hills, the way to the Village of Treadwell presents nothing extraordinary. The state road is worn, winding, with sharp corners, blind driveways, and deer darting across the pavement.

The demand for timeless design ended in the 1800s, with Greek Revival and Victorian clapboard houses replaced by ranch homes with clouded picture windows. The woods are old-growth, with many trees now having lived their natural lives, replaced by "junkers," tenacious young saplings.

Near the village, there are barns and abandoned houses. There is one house, in particular, hidden by discarded trucks, stacks of old tires, rusted refrigerators, and two campers listing missing bumpers and license plates. One sits on worn rims.

Next to it, there is a dark outbuilding without a door. Goats run the manor. Chickens and ducks move in flux in the yard, sometimes littering the road. NRA and "Trump in 2020"signs still hang, three years after. The signs are mud-spattered by cars passing slow rigs, bad decisions, on their on their way to the nearest town.

Trash is strewn across the yard, broken bicycles, and farm equipment broken since the Great Depression. A backyard above ground pool is in the front yard. Like all things on the property, and its parts, it is dirty and busted.

Closer in, you spin into the village, and speed limit slow. Houses wear dresses more finely fit. Scrubby untended lots got swallowed by opulence. Brightly painted doors donning rings of seasonal wreaths. Parks of plantings, ornamental bushes, finely wrought wooden barrels with petunias. Costly Christmas decor scattered down Main Street. Light poles signaling the season.

The river, its water running behind deep-set backyards, sparkles. Bluestone slate sidewalks take over from the pauper's tire-rutted shoulders.

Half a mile's difference delineates two distinct worlds. A cemetery gate severs the village — a copper fountain stained by a green-oxide patina and a broadside begging for donations. The Episcopal Church is rough-cut stone, with arts and crafts windows, and its copper roof catches bouncing light. Subarus nest in the neat driveways.

But the sky is cerulean. Sunsets expire in pink-purple-and orange and neighbors retire from their labors on porches. A tiny village, devoid of traffic.

At night, the sky is dark but owned by stars. Pond peepers singing all night. By nine homes are dark or tinged by television. The surrounding hills hug the village close and protect it.

It's close to pure country, curated by nature but not improved over long-passed time. Doctors and dogs, whether on clear days or not, greet each other and speak as equals.

Cloud Studies 1 & 2

1

Hello, Honey! I'm home! Where are you?
I begin looking for my
cloud climatologist-my husband.
His head jaunts around Jupiter,
so I look there first.
Three layers: ammonia, hydrogen sulfide-
water on the bottom. My eyes weighted by water,
constantly drizzling but not there.

Next, I check Venus. Filled
with sulfuric acid. A day in Los Angeles,
a perpetual haze. Squinting, I don't see him.

Finally falling, back to Earth, I find him.
He's here, cloud gazing, creating elephants out of the heavens,
faces from fog.

2

Pregnant clouds loom,
portending rain.
Greys, browns, smudged.

My NASA scientist sees it. The resident cloud specialist.
He prizes this piece, prays to the artist.
–Lighting is wrong. Brown shades look like dust storm.
England isn't eaten by dust storms.

I don't like where this is going.
Instead, I imagine historical settings.
Dust be damned.
Beethoven lives, thunderous himself.

And Poe's still depressed. Hans Christian Anderson's
tykes still terrified. Mary Shelly miscarried her monsters.

Navier-Stokes fundamental equations of fluid dynamics,
turbulence, again. Constable knows
it's provocative to postulate. My NASA guy glows, as I
study the floor.

Steamboats shear the English Channel,
its sulfurous steam browns the sky.

I understand the nature of light,
Faraday's electromagnetic waves wave.
Fresnel finds waves transverse, side-to-side
Constable senses the theatrics of light and waves.

Mrs. Potato Head

Unaccountable how you usurped elbow,
tracked and stamped your potato-head stamp all over
my freshly washed floor.

Throwing unwieldy weight, you've unbolted
my brush beyond boundaries.

Potato PKA print whether starchy nervous system
or primitive plant, you muddle my mind
with your ghostly tracks. You were here, then faded away,
leaving only your tracks.

Nebra Sky Disc

Blistered disc, pocked and erupted.
A boy-man's moon burnt.
A sailor nervously gnaws metal,
eating the bronze edges.

A mouse in an ocean musing, steering silently.
Crumpled inward, a coined planet.
Dimensions but not directions divined.

Slivered moon, a thumbnail
stars sail searching skies in the sea.
Ancients date that disc.

Moving

Vermont-yanked, uprooted
from there, once growing nicely.
Replanted, transplanted in Indiana.
Father calls it Crawfords*vile*.

What the Feds need, there we go.
Government gives us direction and
destination. Strangers pack our lives.
Movers who disappear on a 3-day drunk.

They never tried to find my bike.
Never sniffed out my stuff.
Gone, gone, gone.
Drunken driver.

Strange language spoken-*warsh rag,
pop, Pee-roo, Ver-sales, French Lick.*

Three years of a young life lost,
yearning to get my bike back.

The ISCCP Conference
(International Satellite Cloud Climatology Project)
Benjamin's Recounting

They, nearly all, wore glasses.
They had visible/invisible pocket protectors.
They wore tweed with patched elbows, blue wool sports coats, kakis/
jeans.
No one smoked. American, Brazilian, English, French,
German, Japanese. One year there were Chinese.
They brought calculators.
They brought acetate slides.
They had military buzz cuts, shoulder-length hair, bald,
wore facial hair.
Talked science, "shop talk" sports, funding, other science.
They work in labs, on military bases, for NASA, NOAA,
maybe the CIA, WMO, The UN, at universities.
They drink too much, they only drink water,
they bring food from home,
they blow out expense accounts.
They came alone, with spouses, partners, colleagues,
who knows who.
They stood in corridors hoping to say hello,
always off dealing with a crisis,
didn't bring a change of clothes.
Mansplained to men,
to their grad students,
to their post docs, to the servers.
They returned to their cliques,
they were loners, they sought new colleagues.
They had to go to another meeting,
they had to get home.

Living Room

Rented apartment, furnished.
Million reasons to throw
throws over everything.
Pray Mom never visits.

Immortal rocker outlives
us all.

Select roses, pinning one in
hair. Campy Andy even then.
No lawn, concrete cracks,
blacktopped, patched
parking lot.

Mink or faux fox fur,
Asian volcano poster posted.
Lonely cross atop mantle.

Detritus of studies, crochet
doilies landladies lame
attempt to make it homey.
Shades aslant, wallpaper
wall-eyed, peeling.

Nuns in an Egg

Never underestimate the power of prayer.
Don't brandish threats; you'll get it all backward.
Contradicting the right way.

Pocket the euphoria. Make a stateable manifesto,
then sluice it down with diluted vinegar.

Superheroes, stolid sisters praying,
peering out from the crotch of
the broccoli-like tree.

Never ask directions. All will be provided
by a celestial GPS, steering you straight.

Staring at Stars

Transfixed by stars.
Homely night. Venus shines against vacancy.

The tree grows, it is living. It is hopeful,
in the moment, this marvelous minute.

Winking, wild, and wondrous
depression doesn't occlude the scene.
Less haunted eyes accept relief, romance, and remedy.

Gibbous moon, he the artist,
every brush stroke for the moon.

Twinkling, he tumultuous in this moment.

Merce Cunningham

Merce is doing a workshop.
There's clarity of form, coordination of torso, legwork,
rhythmic accuracy, spatial awareness, virtuosity.
Neo-Dadaism. With *me,*
dropout of ballet for beginners.
My body's all wrong for this kind of dance.
I persist. I'm in love with modern dance.
Dances dissolve into thin air, as does music.
What really connects them is that if you put them together,
they can take place in the same time.
I write my friends of my adventure.
Please don't tell me how silly I was.

Someone's Been Here

One of Lucy's favorite places to visit is Howe's lumber store. It's a jumble of parts and pieces. Most of it is a mystery to Lucy, but she loves to browse. Casey, another neighbor, is there. "How are you?" she asks. "Oh, about half," he grins. And then Casey starts telling her about visiting his family's abandoned farm last week.

My Dad's old farm is outside of town. No one's lived there for years. Plywood covers the front door and windows. There are falling down outbuildings. We still keep some old farm equipment out there. It's late February and cold as billy hell. Inexpensive plastic patching on the place, breathing in the wind. It makes a sucking and rattling sound. Still, it works to keep cold air and obnoxious critters out. And every few weeks, I drive over, to check on things. Make sure the place is still standing.

I drive my old truck in and immediately notice disturbed snow. Someone's been here. Illegal. Trouble. I touch my gun, and acid rolls in my gut. And, of course, there's no cell service out here.

Seeing the tracks makes me cranky, and my temper flashes. I can feel the flush of my blood pressure going up. There are rules. No. Trespassing! I'll dig a hole, bury the bastard.

Why can't people mind their business and leave other people's things alone? Too late, I realize it's only my brother, Craig. "Well, what are you doing here?" "How the hell you been?" He hollers back over the wind. It turns out he had the same idea on the same day. What are the chances?

We shake, share coffee, and a smoke.
Casey shakes his head, seems to realize that he should be somewhere else. *Well, good to see you Lucy, you take care, now.*
With that, he gives Lucy a wave and leaves the store, hops into his truck, and drives off.

I Prefer
based on Possiblities by Wislawa Szymborska

I prefer quiet conversations
I prefer reading books in the same room
I prefer Fred & Ginger Making a Beeline
I prefer Ellen Bass to floundering
I prefer people with a dry sense of humor
I prefer brilliant to pretty or handsome
I prefer pumpernickel bagels
I prefer spring to fall
I prefer animals to people—except snakes
I prefer going to bed early
I prefer rain for sleeping
I prefer high- thread count sheets
I prefer Mission to Modern
I prefer sepia to color
I prefer biography to history
I prefer figuring out motives
I prefer iris to daisies
I prefer cats to dogs
I prefer libraries to parks
I prefer walking parks to amusement parks
I prefer theatre to opera
I prefer sunny to cloudy
I prefer snow to brown ground
I prefer bright colors
I prefer France to Portugal
I prefer dark to milk chocolate
I prefer MACs to PCs
I prefer redheads to brunettes
I prefer blue eyes to brown

Dimming Day

View of waterway upstaging all else.
Friction forgotten, damage discussed.
Eastwards, ever facing west.

Slow stroll towards home. Waiter
silently clears the scene.

Menagerie of potted plants snuggles,
roses exhale, vibrations from water laps.
Unleashed deep within sigh.
Hourglass sands slip silently into
dimming day, dusk.

Non-Objective Composition, Flight of an Airplane

Iconic art is perpetual.
Squares, half-circles, worms
placed leaf meal.

Sleep, search generalizations engage in
stones, pebbles.
Certainly not hardboiled,
more like felt-vivid colors,
stapled, sewn.

Boggy pancake, sharp features,
noses cartoonish mouths.

Admit it, things change. Jaws
jump away, a woman's silhouette reveals.

Blue skies, glasses rim, straight unibrow,
building windows become eyes, gauges
gage.

That's for sure.
Caterwauling cacophony of shapes,
shades.

Night Light Garish, 1978

Usual blare of horns, shouts,
taxis disgorging people,
everyone rushing
to catch a curtain.

Night light garish
in shades of orange and black.
Porticos plugged by umbrellas.

It's not London, brasher.
Still, in this city of marquees and taxis,
grungy glamour glows.
Lucy loves working in the theatre.

Sunflowers, Sunshine, Sun

In my memory, the sun always shines. The sky always blue with blousy clouds. The grass is always green and so soft that you can walk barefoot and never find a stone.

The sunflowers shine with crooked teeth. Miniature versions of suns. We camped near the smiling plants. Our house on wheels traveled easily. It wasn't lonely. There were always cousins and neighbors.

Silent, secret languages among children, subtle cues. Talk, the grownups never noticed. The sound of laughter, music, and wine at night.

Mamma made me a beautiful skirt. How I loved twirling, feeling the wind. We danced together until the skirt got tangled, and I fell, giggling.

Maud

Maud lived in a simple house, in a simple way.
Cold made her hands hurt worse.
Sheets so cold they felt wet. Maud
burrowed beneath until
her breath brought warmth.
In the worst nights she wore
hat to bed, next to her husband.
Three black cats piled atop her.
Everything was poor. The eiderdown
pillows had feathers formed into hard rocks
in the corners.

Canadian winters were long and dark. Maud
painted summer year-round.
She loved painting life.
Maud was made of pain
but it never broke her brush.
Brushes held awkwardly,
they understood how
difficult they were to hold.

She'd be astonished if she could see
how many people seek out her
simple home, buy reprints of her art
she once sold for a
Canadian nickel.

NY Movie, Edward Hopper 1939

Peggy, usher, tucked in corner under dark
pink, silk lampshades. She wants to be an
actress.

Broken seat, worn velvet squeaks. Bitten lips,
Bee-stung dark red lipstick. Lizard-skin purses,
placed on laps, just so. Candy wrappers rattle.

Beginning, ending. Frame jitters, jumps in splice.
Robert, the guy who changes reels rocks
back on his heels, tries to keep the jam from vaporizing the
celluloid.

Matinee matrons traipse endlessly,
more to sit than see. Relentless reeling.
Peggy has memorized it all by the second
screening.

Piet Mondrian's Name is an Anagram of 'I Paint Modern'

My arm at night,
a thing studied in a dusty room.
A classroom, a schoolmaster,
I act like a cat.
Dessert bakes stress,
bad credit, no debit.
Clapping my card on the table
reflecting.
"Did you know that eleven plus two = twelve plus one?"

They see, the eyes.
Who said funerals feel fun?
Remote, unrested, a meteor as I throw it.
Remote? Meals for one, alone,
sweep the floor, a handful of helpers,
words wrinkle older and wiser.

A video game demo.
Lad, not so young.
He's an unsung old guy,
coins clinking in his pocket.

Ithaca High School, class of 1969
Inspired by "They" by Nina Bogin

Already arriving.
Reforming old cliques, hanging with new cliques,
or alone.
Entering their adolescence,
recalling glory days.
Reliving the worst years of their lives,
were coming home.
They were returning for a victory lap.
They had new shapes, facelifts,
capped teeth, no teeth, deep lines.
Silently judged, were judged.
Excitedly buzzed
did you see him/her/them?
He's drunk, she's gay. Remember?
What the fuck happened?
How did I miss that one? The one that got
away, who blossomed later?
What was his/her name?
You don't recognize me, do you?
Twenty five, fifty years of drama.
A fire, AIDS, car accident, cancer, murder, bee sting.
He overdosed, went to Harvard, Yale,
went to hell and back, never heard of again.
He's rich, famous. She got so fat!
We got so fat. She hasn't changed a bit.
What was her name? Did you know they got
together? Did you know they split?
They pulled on their spouse's sleeve, saying,
Let's go, let's go.
They opened the doors, the right ones, the wrong ones.

Falling Off A Log

Lucy slammed down the cover of her laptop and turned the air blue with invectives. A diesel truck struggled up the hill across the road from her home. Chainsaws clamored, horrible ripping sounds.

What? Why? She texted her neighbor and friend, Eddy Wilcox. Often, she had to wait hours for Eddy to be within cell service. This time, Eddy answered immediately. "It's Mario. He sold logging rights."

Mario was the guy who owned 350 acres of wood and who lived on Long Island. Eddy said that Mario had some nasty kind of cancer, and he guessed Mario needed money.

Lucy had tears of anger. The guy didn't hear or see or probably even care about the wreckage he was creating. The animals who lived in peace most of the year ran in all directions.

"Why couldn't he just have sold it to us," Lucy asked repeatedly.

Benjamin knew that when Lucy was on a tear, it was best to hunker down and wait for her to exhaust herself. So he stolidly read his *History of Philip and Alexander, Two Generations*. It was about Alexander the Great and his father. "Philip was pretty great, too. He just didn't gallivant all over the world."

"Wish he'd sold to me," she continued. And the sounds of trucks and chainsaws continued for the next several months.

Lucy and Benjamin had never met or even laid eyes on Mario. At this point, it was too late. She slammed drawers and doors.

"I get that he's dying, but does he have to kill everything?"

And Eddy, who plowed the driveway for Mario and checked on his property told her what a hash the loggers were making of the cutting. They left trails crowded with fallen logs and showed no signs of going in to clean up the wreckage. Eddy said he was sure Mario had no idea of the mess and damage. The loggers didn't live in this area and traveled an hour each way to their homes.

There was a wetland at the bottom of the property. Without trees to prevent it, a swamp was now attracting mosquitos. The trucks couldn't drive through the mess to remove the trees, and they were now sitting in water.

Lucy said she couldn't zoom with all the commotion going on. And how could she write for the "Truth and Beauty" weeklong workshop? She tried to turn it into poetry, but it was tough going.

Stingy, greedy
Ebenezer Scrooge from bone
to the bark. *Bah humbug*
to the habitat here.

Melvillian long months,
the rolling tide of
splintering wood.
Shipwrecked by sound.
The shrieking of trees.
Branches broken.
Roots wrenched.
Trees toppled.

As a getaway,
I gaze at a goldfinch.
He quietly bubbles
po-ta-to-chip
po-ta-to-chip
in a clean cadence.

The woods will revive,
regrow on its own.
Twigs sprout and tweak.
Not in my lifetime.
The earth grows to glory,
but not in my lifetime.

Yankee Poem

I believe:
That people will be hurt.
That people will recognize themselves.
That there will be trouble right here in River City.
That I can be unreasonable.
That I have to get things out or bad things happen.
That I am blamed.
That I am yelled at.

I believe:
I'm going to do it anyway.
That I will find Graceland, if not grace.
That I will tell the truth as I know it.
That I am a know-it-all.
That I will often be wrong.
That I will destroy friendships if I tell the truth.
That I will do it anyway.

More Than a Handful

Revisiting

The familiar: the pool of stone steps.
Expecting the acrid smell of us and cigarettes,
the whisper of mothballs.
An emptiness—finally, forty years gone.

The Arts & Crafts doorknob,
the nearly black cedar paneling whitewashed. Furniture etched by Ikea,
clean of human hands.

But the door knocker remains.
The stained-glass sconces still hang. The rooms are smaller, lighter, and
the pantry expanded into a
family room with skylights.
The architect a master of fenestration.

No icebox of pale green,
freezer chest with garden vegetables, frozen, waiting to be overcooked.

I think I hear a Nebraska accent
calling my name.

Cot gone, and with it the scary Cornell plaque
that looked like a wild monster. It's dark shadow kept me in my narrow
bed, afraid to put foot to cold floor.

The house smaller.
It's mine
and not.
Ceilings creeping closer, smaller, as did the people over the years.

There are both older and younger ghosts. You can't see them . Don't look
directly, use
peripheral vision, reflections
from copper pots no longer there.
The mirror that isn't there,
in bubbled, leaded glass.

Green carpet on the stairs vanished,
varnish vanished.

Why did they use *that* color?
Where is the desk with the hidden space for important papers?

I say my thanks and leave them to their Ikea furniture,
to their lives in my past space.

Gazing

Glass is wavy, some panes bubbled.
Makes it fun to look through.
Mum's magnifying glass
on top of magazines and books.
Saturday Evening Post, Redbook, Look.
I've never seen her read a new book
or a library one,
but she's always reading,
reading glass always smeary.

On the table a globe with snowmen
stuck inside. The fluid with bubbles
at the top.
Stiff snowflakes floating,
clumpy with time.

I look through all kinds of glass.
Light from the fireplace wraps the room
in orange flames.
Night so dark here, but occasional cars
light slanting snow.
Tire chains jingle as they pass.

The Creek

I am a barefoot child
wading, playing
floating sticks with
cousins.

Watermelon chills with us.
Creek frigid, roaring.
I'm going deaf, brain pounds
with squeals and shouts of
too many cousins.
Dapples blinding.
The sun peeks.

Someone calls. We come running,
right into view of 8-millimeter camera.
I'm heart-stoppingly natural in a body
that belongs to me.
When do we lose this joy and ease?

The Path

Not really a road, more of a path.
Delaware County rock and reddish dirt
Ground into earth, leading into an
abandoned cemetery.

No car passes here.
Perhaps wagon wheels would work,
but long grass chokes the way.

Bees work Dame's Rocket,
humming vibratory songs.
Sun and wind soft through pines.

It's fine to sink into grass or wade
through myrtle.

Welcome. We don't see many visitors.
I guess we're too far off.
You'd have to know we're here, behind
trees. Some of us have names, others
initials only.

Long forgotten dates.
So far off the path.

Big Baby Dowl

Big Baby Doll (Big Baby Dowl) my favorite.
Her rubber face turned brown, then black.
You don't want her. Look, she's ruined.
I loved her. She was mine.

Her body soft and giving. I hugged her. We
slept, warm and tangled together.
Her feet and hands? I think they were soft.

Parents persisted. One sad day, Big Baby Doll
was taken and deposited at the Hartwick Dump.
I cried.
Didn't matter. I was a prisoner
in the back of the black and white '55 Chevy.

Returned home. Alone.
My room empty without her.
No one to love or understand me.
Bye bye Big Baby Dowl

The Turtle

Father found him by side of the road.
Brought him home.
Backyard resident,
happy to be rescued from traffic.

He looks impossibly old,
long slow eye blinks.
I lay on the grass and watch
him for hours.

He has a beautiful domed shell,
Gold and light brown with funny
swirly ridges. I love to trace the
shell, like tortellini.

He often pulls his head in when
neighborhood kids come to look.
No one speaks quietly. No indoor voice
outside. Voices raised bounce off shafts
of sun.

One morning, I find him smashed.
Tommy said Paddy
leaped on the shell.

Not Paddy's first crime. Not his last.
Paddy later jumped on women, breaking
their spirits.

The Circus

A poster in her kitchen.
"Damn Everything but the Circus."
Loves her poster, loves the circus.

I don't get it. Hate the circus.
Always hated it. Now and when I
was five.

We usually agree on books, politics,
food. Not this time. It smells
horrible. Animal scat, old
popcorn, too-sweet cotton candy,
sweat, perfume.
Sour like in Poppy's shed.

Ghastly clowns. Scary faces,
bodies wrong. Tense and gasping,
tightrope. People fall. Contempt
for fat men in red funny hats.

Mum and Bernie's House, Meridale 1960

Sitting by the frosted pane
scratching at rime.
Breathing it anew.

I put off going upstairs.
Bed so cold even under
piles of heavy quilts
sewn by relatives with
unlikely names– Maranah,
Germaine, Rilla, Thankful.

My breath stands out up there,
terribly dark,
sleeping in my knitted hat.

Did the quilters sleep
in these sagging beds?
Did anyone die here?

I pull the quilts over my head
until my breath warms me
and I fall into deep, dark sleep.

Out in the Raised Beds

Scissors sweeping, clipping,
cutting the last herbs
for this year.

Snow early,
herbs half-frozen.
So are my tears.

Protecting them not a
Priority. Didn't catch them
from the cold, the frost, the
storm.

*You did what you could;
they're perennials. That's
what they do*, says my
husband.
Case closed.

I deny this proclamation
from he who has never
gardened.

How could I desert
the plants I grew and
nurtured?

Three Easy Pieces

Maxx sleeps on chair back
deep purrs and noisy breathing
she's dreaming chipmunks

Spring flowers line the drive
forget-me-nots, peonies,
my mailman waving

Rural sky bright blue
Pine boughs in murmuration
childhood remembrance

Beside the Night Stand

At daybreak
the large cat -
Jake -
    Reached down
Under the bed - dust and bottle caps,
    Under the white
eiderdown,
        And dragged out,
 A mouse;
    it was like a small toy

and, blessedly,
    it was dead.
        Jake
Examined the

tiny soft brown body and then
    expertly
        tackled
  Its delicate body,

tossing it and
tossing it back before   crunching it.
    And during this time

the light was growing brighter.
    When I spoke his name
        Jake simply glanced at me.
            White flecked around the muzzle

and with soft glance
    he, too, if you can see it
        had a face like the mouse; and then it was daylight

which had been dawning all the while anyway
    sun broke
        clear of the pines and dropped its bloody pink light
over everything.

Deer in the Drive

Coming back from my mailbox,
I am reading my mail, startled by deer in the drive.

We pause, nod our heads hello.
Please don't run away — I may have an apple here.

That suits her. She stops and watches,
nods, eyes on me, hopeful tongue.

Origami

It arrives in a beautiful square stack of Japanese patterns,
block print, indigo blue, traditional waves, orange and green koi fish
on the reverse side, intense complementary hues
here is where I will write my Reiki prayers.

The accompanying book is for beginners.
Make a crane, a cup to hold wishes, a house to shelter in, a kite to fly.
Fold the corners of the paper sharply.

Reiki prayer papers to protect those I love,
friends who need an embrace —
we have to settle for creased paper wishes.

Folded, they sit in a bowl, those wishes and prayers, a place to focus.
I stir it when I pass.
It's something on the back burner of my mind.

If only I could place my hands on your shoulders, hold your hand,
share my life energy with you, fold you in a pinwheel of love.
I go outside and touch my flowers and wish it was you.

One day we're here, the next day we're gone.
Primary colors, primitive wishes to be turned into beautiful, comforting
shapes.

In this strange time of Origami instead of vaccine, I wish us safety and
health.
We fold ourselves into shapes of comfort and recognition.

I write a prayer on the back of each sheet and stir my bowl.
The paper and ink are often too dark to see what's written.
It's there, gently simmering, folding and unfolding.

And When It's Over

And when it's over,
we learn something,
fly to our former ways?

We will be changed
on a cellular level — our different
DNA passes to the future.

Left with incredulity —
for more than 59 years, I imagine
my end losing my memory.
I live with it.
And now, now I waste so much.

And when it's over, I remember
this *aha* moment.

See, my husband says,
such a terrible waste of time.
Come and kiss your cats.

Three More Haiku

Iris colors flaunt,
hues are vast in range, and they
now stand in straight lines

Only trees speak here
I visit you in my mind
Graveyard whispers hushed

Dog rolls the meadow,
under paw, wild strawberry —
burst of sweet red juice

The Best Advice

August of 1969:
time for me to leave,
my first year of college.

Hugging my grandmother goodbye,
impatient to go.

Her spine bent.
Hands swollen and joints distorted,
she slowly let me go.

*Just one thing — study hard, choose your friends carefully,
and don't forget — more than a handful is sinful.*

What could she know?
A woman who lived
in a too-small dying hamlet,
self-educated, Presbyterian, humble
and uncool.

Fifty years later, not
a single case defies her
best advice.

Acknowledgments

On my return to poetry after several decades away, so many wonderful poets and teachers inspired me. To list everyone would be nauseatingly lengthy, and to forget someone is a sin.

Much gratitude goes to my editor and publisher, Charles Clifford Brooks, III. Cliff shows enduring trust, wonderful humor, and gives me so many opportunities to stretch as a poet and a writer.

Great thanks to Kaitlyn Young for her beautiful design of the cover for *Shoes for Lucy* and for her artistic work with *The Blue Mountain Review*.

Special appreciation to Robert Bensen, mentor, and editor. And to Woodland Arts Editions (Oneonta, NY) for publishing my chapbook, *More Than a Handful* in 2020. They have permitted me to wear those poems again, and so it's tied to the end of *Shoes for Lucy*.

To William Rossow, for his love and support. We've been walking together for fifty years. Most of the time, he keeps me out of the ditches.

www.ingramcontent.com/pod-product-compliance
Lightning Source LLC
Chambersburg PA
CBHW071402080526
44587CB00017B/3158